The Good Granny Diary 2007

Jane Fearnley-Whittingstall

Illustrations by Alex Fox

Published in 2006 by
Short Books
3A Exmouth Mkt
Pine Street
London
EC1R 0JH

10 9 8 7 6 5 4 3 2 1

A CIP catalogue record for this book
is available from the British Library.

Illustration Copyright ©
Alex Fox

ISBN 1-904977-69-3
(978-1-904977-69-8)

Printed in Great Britain by
Butler & Tanner, Frome and London

Jacket Illustration: Alex Fox

Opposite: Picture by Frankie Baldwin, Words by Tommy Mount

I love my granny
because she gives
me biscuits.

	Jan	Feb	Mar	Apr	May	Jun
M	1					
Tu	2				1	
W	3				2	
Th	4	1	1		3	
F	5	2	2		4	1
Sa	6	3	3		5	2
Su	7	4	4	1	6	3
M	8	5	5	2	7	4
Tu	9	6	6	3	8	5
W	10	7	7	4	9	6
Th	11	8	8	5	10	7
F	12	9	9	6	11	8
Sa	13	10	10	7	12	9
Su	14	11	11	8	13	10
M	15	12	12	9	14	11
Tu	16	13	13	10	15	12
W	17	14	14	11	16	13
Th	18	15	15	12	17	14
F	19	16	16	13	18	15
Sa	20	17	17	14	19	16
Su	21	18	18	15	20	17
M	22	19	19	16	21	18
Tu	23	20	20	17	22	19
W	24	21	21	18	23	20
Th	25	22	22	19	24	21
F	26	23	23	20	25	22
Sa	27	24	24	21	26	23
Su	28	25	25	22	27	24
M	29	26	26	23	28	25
Tu	30	27	27	24	29	26
W	31	28	28	25	30	27
Th			29	26	31	28
F			30	27		29
Sa			31	28		30
Su				29		
M				30		
Tu						

2007 Planner

Jul	Aug	Sep	Oct	Nov	Dec	
			1			M
			2			Tu
	1		3			W
	2		4	1		Th
	3		5	2		F
	4	1	6	3	1	Sa
1	5	2	7	4	2	Su
2	6	3	8	5	3	M
3	7	4	9	6	4	Tu
4	8	5	10	7	5	W
5	9	6	11	8	6	Th
6	10	7	12	9	7	F
7	11	8	13	10	8	Sa
8	12	9	14	11	9	Su
9	13	10	15	12	10	M
10	14	11	16	13	11	Tu
11	15	12	17	14	12	W
12	16	13	18	15	13	Th
13	17	14	19	16	14	F
14	18	15	20	17	15	Sa
15	19	16	21	18	16	Su
16	20	17	22	19	17	M
17	21	18	23	20	18	Tu
18	22	19	24	21	19	W
19	23	20	25	22	20	Th
20	24	21	26	23	21	F
21	25	22	27	24	22	Sa
22	26	23	28	25	23	Su
23	27	24	29	26	24	M
24	28	25	30	27	25	Tu
25	29	26	31	28	26	W
26	30	27		29	27	Th
27	31	28		30	28	F
28		29			29	Sa
29		30			30	Su
30					31	M
31						Tu

	Jan	Feb	Mar	Apr	May	Jun
M						
Tu	1			1		
W	2			2		
Th	3			3	1	
F	4	1		4	2	
Sa	5	2	1	5	3	
Su	6	3	2	6	4	1
M	7	4	3	7	5	2
Tu	8	5	4	8	6	3
W	9	6	5	9	7	4
Th	10	7	6	10	8	5
F	11	8	7	11	9	6
Sa	12	9	8	12	10	7
Su	13	10	9	13	11	8
M	14	11	10	14	12	9
Tu	15	12	11	15	13	10
W	16	13	12	16	14	11
Th	17	14	13	17	15	12
F	18	15	14	18	16	13
Sa	19	16	15	19	17	14
Su	20	17	16	20	18	15
M	21	18	17	21	19	16
Tu	22	19	18	22	20	17
W	23	20	19	23	21	18
Th	24	21	20	24	22	19
F	25	22	21	25	23	20
Sa	26	23	22	26	24	21
Su	27	24	23	27	25	22
M	28	25	24	28	26	23
Tu	29	26	25	29	27	24
W	30	27	26	30	28	25
Th	31	28	27		29	26
F		29	28		30	27
Sa			29		31	28
Su			30			29
M			31			30
Tu						

2008 Planner

Jul	Aug	Sep	Oct	Nov	Dec	
		1			1	M
1		2			2	Tu
2		3	1		3	W
3		4	2		4	Th
4	1	5	3		5	F
5	2	6	4	1	6	Sa
6	3	7	5	2	7	Su
7	4	8	6	3	8	M
8	5	9	7	4	9	Tu
9	6	10	8	5	10	W
10	7	11	9	6	11	Th
11	8	12	10	7	12	F
12	9	13	11	8	13	Sa
13	10	14	12	9	14	Su
14	11	15	13	10	15	M
15	12	16	14	11	16	Tu
16	13	17	15	12	17	W
17	14	18	16	13	18	Th
18	15	19	17	14	19	F
19	16	20	18	15	20	Sa
20	17	21	19	16	21	Su
21	18	22	20	17	22	M
22	19	23	21	18	23	Tu
23	20	24	22	19	24	W
24	21	25	23	20	25	Th
25	22	26	24	21	26	F
26	23	27	25	22	27	Sa
27	24	28	26	23	28	Su
28	25	29	27	24	29	M
29	26	30	28	25	30	Tu
30	27		29	26	31	W
31	28		30	27		Th
	29		31	28		F
	30			29		Sa
	31			30		Su
						M
						Tu

Personal data

In case of emergency

Family birthdays and anniversaries

Names and addresses

Goodgranny.com

Our very own site, designed to inform and entertain grandparents and bring them together in the Talk Forum. Log on for news, advice, recipes, gardening tips and our Shop where you can buy presents for your grandchildren and craft kits to make with them.

Mumsnet.com

If you want to know your daughter's and daughter-in-law's ideas about child-rearing and many other subjects including mothers-in-law, this is where you will find them. Also lots of ideas for outings with children and shopping for them.

Rhs.org.uk

The Royal Horticultural Society has several gardens to visit, up and down the country. They sometimes have special events designed for children and families to participate.

Ngs.org.uk

The National Gardens Scheme, better known as The Yellow Book, lists private gardens open for charity. Most are child-friendly and many welcome picnickers. You will almost certainly find one to visit in striking distance every weekend from snowdrop time through to autumn.

BBC.co.uk/cbeebies

Download pictures of your grandchildren's favourite TV characters for the children to colour in. They can also play interactive games online.

English-heritage.org.uk/events

English Heritage has put together trails and events for children and families at many of their castles and other properties, including Knights' Tournaments, Roaming Romans and Meandering Monks.

Nationaltrust.org.uk

Free Tracker Packs are on offer at National Trust properties, offering fun things to do for the whole family. Packs are available for exploring houses, and others for finding out more about the countryside and environment. The Trust also organizes seasonal activities for children such as Easter Egg Trails.

Ukhrail.uel.ac.uk

A guide to the entire heritage railway scene in the UK and Ireland, including details of special events, trains and operating days from all steam railways. There is sure to be one near you.

Giffordscircus.com
A unique regional, touring show in Gloucestershire, Wiltshire and Hay-on-Wye Festival: "a circus with a difference… uniquely old-fashioned, magical, bohemian performance."

Nationalrail.co.uk
Remember, by booking early online, you can reserve a seat and make greater savings on your fare. National Rail also have special offers from time to time, such as sight-seeing tours of London including a River cruise.

Rhymes.org.uk
This website has the words of every nursery rhyme you ever knew, and quite a few you didn't know. It also explains the historical meaning of many of the rhymes.

Flowerfairies.com
Not everyone's cup of tea, but if you believe little girls are made of sugar and spice and all things nice, and

have a like-minded grand-daughter, you might enjoy this site together.

Pantheon.org
Takes you to Encyclopedia Mythica where you can find out about gods and goddesses, heroes and heroines and folk tales from the mythologies of many different cultures.

Earth.google.com
Google Earth combines satellite imagery and maps to put the world's geographic information at your fingertips. Great fun to do with children: just type in an address and zoom in. Look at your house, neighbourhood, exotic foreign locations, anywhere. You can tilt and rotate the view to see 3D terrain and buildings, and save and share your favourites. Even add your own annotations.

Family/kids National Trust events

WALES

Regional office contact: Heledd Jones
heledd.jones@nationaltrust.org.uk
01492 863400

Colby Woodland Garden
Amroth, Narberth, Pembrokeshire SA67 8PP
01834 811885
Fun things to do in the Woodland Garden, craft activities and competitions.
Easter Trails - Good Friday 6 April - Easter Monday 9 April.
11-3.30 daily.
Thursday Fun Days - Thursday 19 July - Thursday 23 August.
11-3.00.

Tudor Merchants House
Quay Hill, Tenby, Pembrokeshire SA70 7BX
01834 842279
Furnished to recreate the atmosphere of family life in Tudor times.
Hunt the Chick - Good Friday 6 April, Easter Sunday 8 April, Easter Monday 9 April. 11-4.30 daily. (Closed Saturday)

Erdigg
Wrexham LL13 0YT
01978 355314
A completely furnished 18th-century large country house, which offers a unique insight into servants' life, with demonstrations of restored historic machines and horse drawn carriage rides.
Easter trails on Good Friday, Saturday, Sunday and Bank Holiday Monday.
Teddy Bears Picnic on 24th June
The Victorian Festival will be on 4th and 5th Aug.
Apple Festival 6th and 7th October and **Halloween Hootings** on 28th October.

Family/kids National Trust events

NORTH WEST

Penrhyn Castle
Bangor, Gwynedd LL57 4HN
01248 353084
Spectacular 19th-century fantasy castle with dolls museum, extensive Victorian kitchens, railway museum and adventure playground.
Mother's Day luncheon: special Mothering Sunday menu and 20% discount voucher for mothers (and grandmothers) spending £5 in the tea rooms.
Easter Saturday Eggstravaganza: Family fun day with Easter egg trail, face painting and archery. 12-4pm
Toys and Trains Fun Day
Thursday 26 July
Knights and Castles Fun Day
Thursday 23 August
Penrhyn goes Batty, Saturday 27 October: celebrate Halloween with bat trails 12-4pm

Contact: Liz Houseman
Liz.houseman@nationaltrust.org.uk 015394 63810

Beatrix Potter Gallery
Main Street, Hawkshead, Cumbria LA22 0NS 015394 36355
In 2007 the exhibition at the Beatrix Potter Gallery will feature 'The Tale of Tom Kitten', a book which includes many illustrations based on Hill Top Garden. There will be **Easter Trails** at both – April 8&9.

Wordsworth House
Main Street, Cockermouth, Cumbria CA13 9RX
01900 820884
A wonderful insight into the Wordsworths' family life, with costumed interpreters, and interactive demonstrations and tastings in the working kitchen. Lots of items to touch and use including the children's toys.

Family/kids National Trust events

NORTH WEST contd

Mendips (John Lennon's childhood home)
Woolton, Liverpool
0870 900 0256
Experience a unique insight into the life and times of John Lennon as a boy through photographs, docments and other fascinating memorabilia.

EAST OF ENGLAND

Regional Contact: Lynsey Thorpe
lynsey.thorpe@nationaltrust.org.uk
Tel: 01284 747557

Brancaster Millennium Activity Centre, Norfolk
01485 210719
Crafty Days in February half term: By the Seaside. Comb the beach for shells, driftwood and seaweed to incorporate into a shaker stick and puppet. In the Woods. Gather seeds, leaves and bark in the woods and create a mask or mobile to take home. These days are priced at £39 per child (2006 price) to include all tuition and materials. Family Fun Weeks (April and August): Action-packed weeks full of fun activities like sailing, kayaking, cycling, orienteering, beach fun and team building. The weeks are fully residential with all meals, accommodation, tuition and equipment included in the price.

Family/kids National Trust events

The Centre offers a room per family group with en-suite facilities an freshly prepared food. The adults are not expected to take part in the daytime activities (though can if they want to), leaving them free to explore the beautiful countryside and coastline surrounding the Centre. Prices for these weeks range from £148-£221 per person depending on no. of children participating from the same family group. All courses are aimed at children aged 8-14. Booking is essential for all events.

Melford Hall, Suffolk
Long Melford, Sudbury,
Suffolk CO10 9AA
01787 379228
Beatrix Potter Storytelling. A costumed 'Beatrix Potter' tells stories to children in the banqueting house. There is a slightly educational element with the volunteer telling the children about Beatrix's life and connections with the Trust. Age group – under 8yrs. £1 per child. Usually held every Thursday during the summer holidays. Also children's outdoor trails and a mile long walk in the park which is just the right length for grannies and children.

Wimpole Home Farm
Wimpole Hall, Arrington, Royston,
Cambridgeshire
SG8 0BW
01223 206000
18th-century rare breeds farm with sheep, goats, cattle, pigs and horses. Also shire-horse wagon rides and driving courses.

Elizabethan House Museum
4 South Quay, Great Yarmouth,
Norfolk NR30 2QH
01493 855746
Museum of domestic life in a 16th-century house, with lots of hands-on activities and children's playroom filled with toys from the past. Events take place all year round.

SOUTH EAST

Regional contact: Sharon Cadman
Sharon.cadman@nationaltrust.
org.uk
Tel: 01372 455051

Claremont Landscape Garden
Esher, Surrey
Feed the ducks and waterfowl
on the lake. Children's trails,
lots of different holiday
activities.

Sheffield Park Garden
Sheffield Park, East Sussex
TN22 3QX
01825 790231
Internationally renowned 'Capability'
Brown landscaped garden, with
waterfalls, cascades and four large
lakes. Tracker Packs, art palettes,
children's trails.

Petworth House
Petworth, West Sussex
GU28 0AE
01798 342207

Magnificent country house and
park. Tracker Packs, children's
quizzes, see the deer.

Standen
West Hoathly Road, East
Grinstead, West Sussex
RH19 4NE
01342 323029
Arts & Crafts family home with
Morris and Co. interiors, set in a hill-
side garden and offering lovely
orchard and woodland walks.
Tracker Packs, art bags, quizzes.

Knole
Sevenoaks, Kent TN15 0RP
01732 462100
One of England's greatest show
houses, set in a magnificent deer
park. Park activity packs, house trail,
holiday activities.

SOUTH WEST

Bodiam Castle

Bodiam, nr Robertsbridge, East
Sussex TN32 5UA
01580 830436
Perfect example of a late medieval
moated castle. Great for little boys,
with battlements, ramparts and moat
to explore, and an opportunity to try
on armour (ring ahead to check).

Polesden Lacey

nr Dorking, Surrey 01372 452048
Go and have a picnic in the gardens.
There are also outdoor trails and
house quizzes.Plus a nature hide,
Squirrels Corner play area, Tracker
Packs.

Dapdune Wharf

Guildford, Surrey 01483 561389
Go in the restored barge 'Reliance'.
View the interactive exhibitions and
visit the hands-on discovery room in
the Gunpowder Store. Take a boat
trip on the River Wey.

Regional contact: Sharon Cadman
Sharon.cadman@nationaltrust.
org.uk
Tel: 01372 455051

Brownsea Island

Poole, Dorset BH13 7EE
01202 707744
Peaceful island of woodland
and heath with wide variety of
wildlife, with trails for young
smugglers, historians and
explorers.

Kingston Lacy

Wimborne Minster, Dorset
BH21 4EA
01202 883402
Elegant country mansion with
children's adventure playground
Iron Age hill-fort, and Badbury
Rings.

SOUTH WEST contd

Lanhydrock
Bodmin, Cornwall PL30 5AD
01208 265950
Magnificent late-Victorian country
house which has a lovely
adventure playground, with
wobbly bridge, scramble nets
and animal sculptures.

Buckland Abbey
Yelverton, Devon PL20 6EY
01822 853607
700-year-old home of Elizabethan
seafarer Sir Francis Drake. Have
a go at butter-making. Also, don't
miss the Lifetimes Gallery, which
now has Tudor children's clothes
to try on.

NORTHERN IRELAND

Regional contact: Christine Rogers
Christine.rogers@nationaltrust.org.
uk
Tel: 028 97512351

Carrick-a-Rede
119a Whitepark Road, Ballintoy,
Co. Antrim BT54 6LS
028 2076 9839
A rocky island connected to the
cliffs by a rope bridge and a site of
Special Scientific Interest. Here you
can find unique geology, flora and
fauna and fantastic bird-watching.

SCOTLAND

Regional contact:
information@nts.org.uk
Tel: 0131 243 9300

Culzean Castle & Country Park
Maybole, South Ayrshire,
KA19 8LE.
tel 01655 884400
A great place to spend the day.
The castle was converted by the
architect Robert Adam as a
bachelor residence for the Earl of
Cassillis, between 1777 and 1792.
There is an Armoury with an
impressive display of flintlock pistols
and swords. The Swan Pond is the
perfect spot for a family picnic.
There's an adventure playground,
and beaches too.

Craigievar Castle
Alford, Aberdeenshire AB33 8JF,
Tel 013398 83635
Craigievar's Great Tower was built
by Master William Forbes in the

early 17th century.
There are extensive parkland
grounds and a waymarked walk –
the first loop is easy walking
through open woodland which
seems to glow blue in early summer when the bluebells are in
flower.

Brodick Castle, Garden & Country Park
Isle of Arran, KA27 8HY.
Tel 01770 302202
Brodick Castle, its gardens and
country park stretch from the
shore to the highest peak on
Arran. In the country park there are
wildflower meadows where
Highland cows graze, woodland
trails and tumbling waterfalls. And
you can find out about the park's
wildlife at the Countryside Centre.
There's also an exciting adventure
playground.

Birthday present ideas

TODDLERS

★Wooden bricks and a cheap plastic lorry to transport them

★Electric toothbrush

★Toy Hoover

★Snakes and Ladders

★Toy pushchair

★*Easy Peasy* cookbook

OLDER CHILDREN

★Hawsers, cleats and pulleys from a Ship's Chandler

★Second-hand portable manual typewriter

★Table-tennis net with clips to fix it to kitchen or dining-table, plus bats and balls

★A watch on a chain

★A rope ladder

★Dolls' house furniture and accessories – you don't need an expensive dolls' house to put them in: a cardboard box for each room is fine, or just a shelf or windowsill

★A dressing up box: take a battered old suitcase or trunk and fill it with old clothes (silks, velvets, brocade, fake fur), hats, belts, shoes, bangles and beads. If you haven't hoarded your own vintage garments, trawl local charity shops

★A multi-layered wild animal jigsaw (www.georgeluckpuzzles.com)

★Charm bracelet – try and remember to add new charms each birthday

★'Radio Flyer' trolley (from the Outdoor Toy Co)

GRANNY'S TOP DVDs

★*Baby Mozart*

★*Wallace and Gromit –*
   3 Cracking Adventures

★*The Jungle Book*

★*Mary Poppins*

★*Chitty Chitty Bang Bang*

★*Bedknobs & Broomsticks*

★*Shrek 1 and 2*

★*Finding Nemo*

★*The Incredibles*

The following have been tried, tested and loved. Some are classics that are already familiar to you, others are classics of the future:

FOR YOUNGER CHILDREN:

★ *Spot's Touch and Feel Book,* by Eric Hill

★ *The Hungry Caterpillar,* by Eric Carle

★ *You Choose,* by Pippa Goodheart

★ *Each Peach Pear Plum,* by Alan and Janet Ahlberg

★ *Horrid Henry's Big Bad Book,* by Francesca Simon

★ *We're Going on a Bear Hunt,* by Michael Rosen and Helen Oxenbury

★ *Don't Let the Pigeon Drive the Bus,* by Mo Willems

★ *The Gruffalo,* by Julia Donaldson and Axel Scheffler

★ *Where the Wild Things Are,* by Maurice Sendak

★ *The Cock, the Mouse and the Little Red Hen,* illustr. by Graham Percy

FOR OVER 6s:

★ *Fantastic Mr Fox,* by Roald Dahl (indeed any Roald Dahl book)

★ *Our Island Story* (fantastic new, revised edition)

★ *The Secret Garden,* by Frances Hodgson Burnett

★ *Holes,* by Louis Sachar

★ *Carrie's War,* by Nina Bawden

★ *The Wolves of Willoughby Chase,* by Joan Aiken (and sequels)

★ *Pippi Long-stocking,* by Astrid Lindgren

★ *The Wool-pack,* by Cynthia Harnett

★ *Northern Lights,* by Philip Pullman

★ *When Hitler Stole Pink Rabbit,* by Judith Kerr

Metric Conversions

LINEAR

1 inch – 25.4 millimetres
1 foot – 304.8 millimetres
1 yard – 0.91 metre
1 mile – 1.6 kilometres
1 millimetre – 0.039 inch
1 meter – 1.09 yards
1 kilometre – 0.62 mile

SQUARE

1 sq yard – 0.83 sq metre
1 acre – 0.40 hectare
1 sq mile – 2.58 sq kilometres
1 sq metre – 1.19 sq yards
1 hectare – 2.47 acres
1 sq kilometre – 0.38 sq mile

CUBIC

1 cubic foot – 0.028 cubic metre
1 cubic metre – 35.31 cubic feet

VOLUME

1 pint – 0.56 litre
    – 20 fluid ounces
1 litre – 1.75 pints
1 gallon – 4.54 litres

TEMPERATURE

To convert F degrees to C,
deduct 32 and multiply by 5/9
To convert C degrees to F,
multiply by 9/5 and add 32

WEIGHT

1 oz – 28.34 grams
1 lb – 0.45 kilogram
1 cwt – 50.802 kilograms
1 ton – 1.01 tonne

Colour-in Map

For little scribblers

January
2007

January brings the snow,
Makes the feet and fingers glow
Sara Coleridge 1802-52

Twelfth Night

Twelfth night is traditionally the time to take down
Christmas cards and decorations. Small children like to help
dismantling the Christmas tree, look at favourite baubles and
pack them away carefully. Check with your local authority
whether they have a recycling scheme for trees –
some offer a collection service.

The Woodland Trust (www.woodlandtrust.org.uk) recycles cards;
simply take them to your nearest WH Smith or Tesco. Do your own
recycling by saving wrapping paper to cut up for next year's paper
chains, and put ribbons and anything that glitters in your collage box.

1 Monday

2 Tuesday

3 Wednesday   *Full Moon*

4 Thursday

5 Friday

6 Saturday

7 Sunday

Mrs Beeton's Seville Orange Marmalade

1¹/₂lbs Seville oranges
2 pts water
Juice of one lemon
3lbs sugar

Wash the fruit and put it whole and unpeeled into a saucepan.
Pour on two pints of boiling water and simmer gently with the
lid on the pan until the fruit is tender enough to be pierced
easily with a fork (approx. two hours). (Alternatively the whole
fruit and water can be baked in a covered casserole in a cool
oven until the fruit is soft; this will take about four to five
hours). Cut the fruit in half and remove pips, then cut up the
fruit with a knife and fork, carefully retaining all the juice.
Return the pips to the water in which the fruit was cooked,
and boil for five minutes to extract more pectin. Put the sliced
fruit with the liquid (strained free from pips) and lemon juice
in the preserving pan. Reduce the heat, add the sugar and stir
till dissolved. Bring to the boil and boil rapidly till setting
point is reached. Note: This method is simple to do and is
recommended if a fairly coarse-cut marmalade is liked.

8 Monday

9 Tuesday

10 Wednesday

11 Thursday

12 Friday

13 Saturday

1926 Birthday of Michael Bond,
creator of Paddington Bear

14 Sunday

Feed the Birds

with special wild bird seed mixes and
fat balls hung from trees and shrubs.
You can make your own fat balls with the grandchildren:
Melt suet or lard in a saucepan.
Mix in some or all of the following:
bird seed, nuts, oatmeal, dried fruit.
Leave to cool a bit, then pour into yoghurt pots, tea cups or
ramekins. Stick a drinking straw in the middle of each one.
When they are set hard, remove from the mould and
thread string through the hole left by the straw.

The North wind will blow
And we shall have snow,
And what will poor robin do then, poor thing?
He'll sit in the barn
And keep himself warm,
And hide his head under his wing, poor thing.

15 Monday

---

16 Tuesday

---

17 Wednesday

---

18 Thursday

New Moon

---

19 Friday

---

20 Saturday

*20 January-19 February **Aquarius***

---

21 Sunday

Burns Night

The birth of Scotland's national poet is celebrated by Scots at 'Burns Night' dinners all over the world. The menu always features haggis, celebrated in Burns's poem *To a Haggis* as 'Great chieftain of the puddin' race'. Haggis is a mixture of offal, oatmeal and spices stuffed into a sheeps stomach, boiled and served with whisky sauce.

Burns's most famous poem is his adaptation of the folk rhyme *Auld Lang Syne*. Another much-loved poem, *To a Mouse,* begins:

'Wee sleekit cow'rin' timorous beastie,
O what a panic's in thy breastie...
The best laid plans of mice and men
Gang aft aglay,
And leave us nought but grief and pain
For promis'd joy!'

22 Monday

23 Tuesday

24 Wednesday
1965 Winston Churchill died

25 Thursday
1759 Robert Burns's birthday

26 Friday

27 Saturday
1832 Birthday of Charles Dodgson
(Lewis Carroll), author of Alice in
Wonderland and Through the Looking Glass

28 Sunday

Grannyblog

My best friend's grandmother was everything a child could want. Hilariously funny, slightly rakish (introduced us to sherry in the afternoon age 14) but solidly grandmotherly – would entertain us kiddies in her huge house with wonderful food and much loving attention and constant stream of running jokes. I think of her quite a lot and if I had any role model it would most certainly be her.

It's important not to let your daughter think you are more interested in the children than in her life and interests, and to respect and appreciate all she does.

It's great being a Grandma. I only wish I lived a little closer to them all.

Children need to learn that grandparents get tired.

My mother adored her grandchildren and spoilt them a bit, she was wonderfully generous and would always look after them. She made them dainty sandwiches and pretty cakes and they loved her. She also loved playing cards with them.

They love me so much and can talk to me on any subject.

29 Monday

30 Tuesday

31 Wednesday

February
2007

The man in the moon
Came down too soon
And asked his way to Norwich.
They told him South
And he burnt his mouth
With eating cold pease porridge.

The Moon

Hey diddle diddle
The cat and the fiddle,
The cow jumped over the moon.
The little dog laughed to see such fun,
And the dish ran away with the spoon.

Sow peas and beans in the wane of the moone,
Who soweth them sooner, he soweth too soon.
Five Hundred Points of
Goode Husbandry by Thomas Tusser

Small boys love facts.
Here are some about the moon:
Its maximum daily temperature is 230F (110C)
Its minimum daily temperature is 292F (-180C)
The moon's diameter is 2,160 miles.
It is 239,000 miles from Earth.

February 2007

1 Thursday   *Full Moon*

2 Friday   *1650 Nell Gwyn's birthday*

3 Saturday

4 Sunday

In the Garden

Cut branches of hazel catkins and forsythia and show your grandchildren how the buds open indoors. Enjoy the flowers of Daphne mezereum, winter jasmine, winter aconites, snowdrops and Iris unguicularis. If you don't grow them, you can buy snowdrop and aconite bulbs now, 'in the green'. Even in the smallest plot there's always room for a few more bulbs.

Snowdrop fans or *galanthophiles* are out and about, feasting their eyes (and noses – did you know some snowdrops are scented?). Many gardens and estates with spectacular displays of snowdrops have special openings in February. Check the local press, the Yellow Book (www. Ngs.org.uk), The National Trust or your county Wildlife Trust for where to go.

February 2007

5 Monday

6 Tuesday   *1665 Queen Anne's birthday*

7 Wednesday

8 Thursday

9 Friday

10 Saturday

11 Sunday   *1800 birthday of Henry Fox Talbot,*
                                 pioneer of photography

Get the children to draw or paint Valentine cards, or make collage hearts.

Invest in a heart-shaped biscuit cutter and make Valentine biscuits with pink and white icing or cut out heart-shaped sandwiches made with thin-sliced white bread with your grandchildren's favourite fillings.

Painting by Oscar, 6

12 Monday

13 Tuesday

14 Wednesday   *Valentine's day*

15 Thursday

16 Friday

17 Saturday

18 Sunday

Pancake Day

Pancakes are traditionally eaten on Shrove Tuesday, and in some places pancake races are held. The oldest, at Olney near Milton Keynes, was first run in 1445. The story goes that a woman was cooking her pancakes when she heard the bells of St Peter's and St Paul's Church summoning her to prayer. She rushed out of the house with her frying pan in her hand, still wearing her apron.

PANCAKE BATTER

8 oz plain flour, salt, 2 eggs, 1 pint milk.
Sift flour and salt into a bowl, make a well in the centre and break eggs into it. Add a splash of milk and beat with a wire or electric whisk till smooth, adding more milk if needed. Stir in the rest of the milk and stand for 30 mins. Heat a (non-stick) frying pan, grease lightly with butter or oil and pour in enough batter to just cover the pan. When the batter looks set, turn it using a palette knife. Spread with your favourite filling, folded or rolled up. If you let your grand-children have a go at tossing their pancakes, be prepared to scrape them off the floor or ceiling (the pancakes, not the children)!

19 Monday

20 Tuesday

20 February-20 March **Pisces**
Shrove Tuesday

21 Wednesday

22 Thursday

23 Friday

24 Saturday

25 Sunday

Tweedledum and Tweedledee

Tweedledum and Tweedledee
Agreed to have a battle;
For Tweedledum said Tweedledee
Had spoiled his nice new rattle.

Just then flew down a monstrous crow
As black as a tar-barrel;
which frightened both the heroes so,
They quite forgot their quarrel.
Alice's Adventures in Wonderland, by Lewis Carroll

26 Monday

27 Tuesday

28 Wednesday

*1820 Birthday of Sir John Tenniel,
illustrator of Alice in Wonderland*

N.B. Grandparents get enormous pleasure out of seeing
their grandchildren read books they loved when they
themselves were children. Keep a stock of your own
favourites to read to them at bedtime, and give them tapes
to listen to in the car. Start with Beatrix Potter and go on to
Lewis Carroll's *Alice in Wonderland* and *Through the looking
Glass*, Kenneth Grahame's *The Wind in the Willows* and
Kipling's *Just so Stories*. The choice is yours. Once you have
made the introduction they will end up reading to
themselves, and quoting their favourite bits back to you.

March
2007

It was a lover and his lass,
With a hey, and a ho, and a hey nonino,
That o'er the green cornfield did pass,
In the spring time, the only pretty ring time,
When birds do sing, hey ding a ding, ding;
Sweet lovers love the spring.
As You Like It, by William Shakespeare

St David

St David – or, in Welsh, Dewi Sant – is the patron
saint of Wales. As Archbishop of Wales he preached
Christianity to the Celtic tribes in the 6th century.
St David's Day is also the National Day of Wales.
The national emblems are a leek and a daffodil.
Passionate nationalists have been known to wear
leeks on their lapels on St David's Day, but
a daffodil in the buttonhole is more usual.

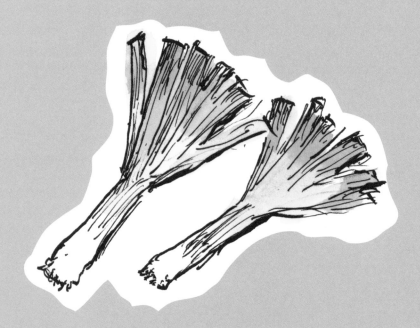

LEEK AND POTATO SOUP

Slice 1 lb leeks into $^1/_2$ inch lengths and soften in 1 oz butter.
Add 12 oz potatoes, peeled and cubed, and 1 pint good chicken
stock. Bring to the boil and simmer until tender. Whizz in
the blender until smooth. If the mixture is too thick, add
more stock or milk. Heat, season and serve with
croutons or crumbled crispy bacon.

---

1 Thursday *St David's Day*

---

2 Friday

---

3 Saturday *Full Moon*

---

4 Sunday

Spring Cleaning

The Wind in the Willows by Kenneth Graham 1959-1932

The mole had been working very hard all the morning, spring cleaning his little home. First with brooms, then with dusters; then on ladders and steps and chairs, with a brush and a pail of whitewash; till he had dust in his throat and eyes, and splashes of whitewash all over his black fur, and an aching back and weary arms. Spring was moving in the air above and in the earth below and around him, penetrating even his dark and lowly little house with its spirit of divine discontent and longing. It was small wonder, then, that he suddenly flung down his brush on the floor, said "Bother!" and "Oh blow!" and also "Hang spring cleaning!" and bolted out of the house without even waiting to put on his coat.

March 2007

5 Monday

6 Tuesday

7 Wednesday
1876 Alexander Graham Bell patented his new invention, the telephone

8 Thursday
1859 Kenneth Grahame born, author of The Wind in the Willows.

9 Friday

10 Saturday

11 Sunday

Simnel Cake
Traditionally baked for Mothering Sunday

The marzipan: first make a big ball of marzipan. In a large mixing bowl, combine 350g ground almonds with 250g icing sugar. Add 1 tbs lemon juice, then 3 beaten egg yolks, a little at a time, and maybe not all of it, working the mix with your hands to get a stiff paste that won't crack later. Wrap in clingfilm and set aside. *The cake:* sift 250g plain flour with $1/2$ tsp salt, 2 level tsp baking powder and 1 level tsp grd mixed spice. Cream 200g soft unsalted butter with 200g light brown sugar until light and airy. Beat in 3 eggs, one at a time, adding 1 tbs sifted flour mix after each egg. Fold in the remaining flour, alternately with the juice of 1 lemon and $1/2$ orange. Then fold in 200g each of currants, raisins and sultanas, 125g chopped mixed candy peel (optional) and the finely grated zest of 1 orange and 1 lemon. Mix thoroughly. Pile half the mixture into a lined and greased, high-sided, 20cm cake tin, then level the top. Make a ball of a little less than half the marzipan and press or roll it out to a circle that fits snugly in the tin. Lay this over the cake mixture, then spread the second half of the mixture on top. Bake in the centre of a fairly low oven (150°C/gas mark 2) for 2 to $2^{1}/2$ hours, until the top is golden brown and a knife blade pushed into the centre comes out clean. Leave to cool in the tin. Turn out of the tin and brush the top with a little melted jam. Roll out the remaining marzipan into a neat circle and lay it over the top of the cake. Flash under a hot grill to get a lightly toasted surface, then leave to cool again. Now let your grandchildren decorate it!

12 Monday

---

13 Tuesday

---

14 Wednesday

---

15 Thursday   *The Ides of March, assassination of*
                               Julius Caesar 44BC

---

16 Friday

---

17 Saturday   *St Patrick's Day*

---

18 Sunday   *New moon,*
                                                  Mothers Day UK

Vera Lynn

'The Forces Sweetheart' during World War II, and later made a Dame, she sang many hits including:

WHITE CLIFFS OF DOVER

There'll be blue birds over
The white cliffs of Dover,
Tomorrow, just you wait and see.
There'll be love and laughter,
And peace ever after,
Tomorrow when the world is free.

The shepherd will tend his sheep,
The valley will bloom again.
And Jimmy will go to sleep,
In his own little room again.

Spring Festival at Kew Gardens
From 17 March to 15 April, this includes the crocus carpet, a million bulbs, trees in blossom. Also 'Climbers and Creepers', an interactive play zone much loved by small children, is always open. Take a picnic.

19 Monday

20 Tuesday

1917 Vera Lynn's birthday

21 Wednesday

21 March – 20 April **Aries**

22 Thursday

23 Friday

24 Saturday

25 Sunday

British summer time begins.
Put clocks forward 1 hour. Less sleep.

Have Your Own Boat Race

To make a paper boat:

1. Take an A4 sheet of paper.

2. Fold it in half.

3. Fold the top corners E and F to the centre.

4. Fold the flap A-B up. Turn over and do the same with flap C-D. Then open out from the centre and flatten into diamond shape.

5 & 6. Fold up the AB point as shown. turn over and fold up the CD point.

7 & 8 Put your fingers into the centre and pull the two pointed ends gently apart, at the same time folding both sides up, coaxing it into the shape of a boat.

9. Make lots more and organise a naval battle on a pond or in the bath.

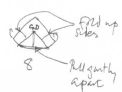

March 2007

26 Monday

27 Tuesday

28 Wednesday

In the Oxford and Cambridge Boat Race of 1912, both boats sank.

29 Thursday

30 Friday

31 Saturday

Home-thoughts from Abroad
O to be in England
Now that April's there,
And whoever wakes in England
See, some morning, unaware,
That the lowest boughs and the brushwood sheaf
Round the elm-tree bole are in tiny leaf,
While the chaffinch sings on the orchard bough
In England – now!
Robert Browning
1812-1889

April
2007

I was a war baby (World War II, not I, in case you wondered) and we didn't have chocolate Easter eggs because of food rationing. Instead, our breakfast boiled eggs on Easter morning came brightly coloured.

Your grandchildren can do this easily, if you show them how, and supervise the younger ones. Simply add cochineal or blue, green or yellow food colouring in the water when you boil the eggs. You need quite a lot of colouring, at least a dessertspoon per pint of water. Use white, not brown eggs for the best results. Eggs can also be decorated after boiling, using washable felt-tips. If you hard-boil the eggs you can hide them in the garden for an Easter-egg hunt.

1 Sunday   *April Fool's Day*

Daffodils

William Wordsworth 1770-1850

I wander'd lonely as a cloud
That floats on high o'er vales and hills,
When all at once I saw a crowd
A host, of golden daffodils;
Beside the lake, beneath the trees,
Fluttering and dancing in the breeze.

Continuous as the stars that shine
And twinkle on the milky way,
This stretch'd in never-ending line
Along the margin of the bay:
Ten thousand saw I at a glance,
Tossing their heads in spritely dance.

The waves beside them danced, but they
Out-did the sparkling waves in glee:
A poet could not but be gay,
In such a jocund company:
I gazed – and gazed – but little thought
What wealth the show to me had brought:

For oft, when on my couch I lie
In vacant or in pensive mood,
They flash upon that inward eye
Which is the bliss of solitude;
And then my heart with pleasure fills,
And dances with the daffodils.

April 2007

2 Monday — *Full Moon*

3 Tuesday

4 Wednesday

5 Thursday

6 Friday — *Good Friday*

7 Saturday — *Easter Saturday*
1770 William Wordsworth born

8 Sunday — *Easter Day*

Grannyblog

They are so loving to us, so sweet and charming and interesting. I'm potty about them.

I love having them each to stay on their own. I had a brilliant day out with a six-year-old grandson to the Tower of London.

I believe grandchildren bring families together and create a wonderful family unit.

It is so much easier to be a grandparent than a parent – easier now to stand back and not get caught up in the 'drama.'

I had a very close relationship with my maternal grandmother: she and my step-grandfather lived next door and I saw them every day. When I came in from school I went straight to Granny because I loved her cakes and tea better than Mum's! She taught me masses – games, about books, the garden, how to tell the time – a major contribution to my life.

9 April, 1806 – Isambard Kingdom Brunel's birthday. Engineer of the Great Western Railway including 2-mile-long Box Tunnel, and of the steamships Great Western and Great Britain. A visit to SS Great Britain at Bristol docks makes a great outing for grandchildren. See www.ssgreatbritain.org

9 Monday

10 Tuesday

11 Wednesday

12 Thursday

13 Friday

14 Saturday

15 Sunday

The Queen's Birthday

Queen Elizabeth was born in 1926 at 17 Bruton Street in
Mayfair, London, and baptized Elizabeth Alexandra Mary,
after her mother, the Duchess of York, her great-grandmother
Queen Alexandra and her grandmother Queen Mary. She is
81 this year, and is said to be close to her seven grandchildren.
They are:

PRINCE WILLIAM OF WALES
born 1982

PRINCE HARRY OF WALES
born 1984

PETER PHILLIPS
born 1977

ZARA PHILLIPS
born 1981

PRINCESS BEATRICE OF YORK
born 1988

PRINCESS EUGENIE OF YORK
born 1990

THE LADY LOUISE WINDSOR
born 2003

16 Monday

17 Tuesday

New Moon

18 Wednesday

19 Thursday

20 Friday

21 Saturday

*21 April – 21 May **Taurus***
Queen Elizabeth's birthday

22 Sunday

St George and the Dragon

St George probably never came to England, although he is its patron saint. His legend tells of how the city of Silene in Libya was threatened by a pestilential dragon which would only be appeased by the gift every day of a beautiful maiden to devour. When it was the turn of the king's lovely young daughter Cleodolinda, she was about to be eaten when a brave knight galloped up on a white horse, wearing a red cross on his white tunic. After a long battle St George finally wounded the monster. He put the princess's girdle around its neck and she led the dragon, now quite docile, triumphantly into the city.

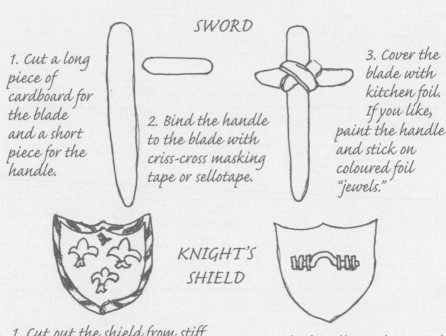

SWORD

1. Cut a long piece of cardboard for the blade and a short piece for the handle.

2. Bind the handle to the blade with criss-cross masking tape or sellotape.

3. Cover the blade with kitchen foil. If you like, paint the handle and stick on coloured foil "jewels."

KNIGHT'S SHIELD

1. Cut out the shield from stiff cardboard and paint it with a heraldic design.

2. For the handle, stick or staple a loop of cardboard on the back.

23 Monday

24 Tuesday

25 Wednesday

26 Thursday

27 Friday

28 Saturday

*28-30: Woodland Wonders
Festival at Kew Gardens*

29 Sunday

1769 The Duke of Wellington born

In the Garden

March winds, April showers
Bring forth May flowers.

Now that the earth has warmed up a bit, seeds will germinate and grow quickly. Sow them straight into the ground or, if you prefer, in pots or seed trays. If gardening is your passion, as it is mine, you might want to encourage your grandchildren to share it by giving them their own set of garden tools to keep at your place, together with an apron and a pair of wellies. If you don't mind a bit of a mess, toddlers are very happy digging in any empty patch of earth. Large seeds like peas (and sweet peas), beans, marigolds and nasturtiums are easy for them to handle. For quickest results sow *Limnanthes douglasii* (poached egg flower, 13 weeks from sowing to flowering) Sweet Alyssum (14 weeks), Cornflower and *Eschscholzia* (15 weeks) and *Calendula* (Pot Marigold 16 weeks). Older children can have their own small plots to grow crops of their choice: radishes and sweetcorn, perhaps, or snapdragons and sunflowers.

30 Monday

Home Thoughts from Abroad *continued...*
And after April, when May follows,
And the whitethroat builds, and all the swallows!
Hark, where my blossom'd pear-tree in the hedge
Leans to the field and scatters on the clover
Blossoms and dewdrops – at the bent spray's edge –
That's the wise thrush; he sings each song twice over,
Lest you should think he never could recapture
The first fine careless rapture!
And though the fields look rough with hoary dew,
All will be gay when noontide wakes anew
The buttercups, the little children's dower
– Far brighter than this gaudy
melon-flower!
Robert Browning
1812-1889

May
2007

Elderflower Cordial

Go for a country walk and pick a basket of elderflowers.

30 elderflower heads
6 pints (approx. 3l) boiling water
2lbs (990g) caster sugar
1 packet of citric acid (available from chemists)
2 unwaxed oranges
3 unwaxed lemons

Gently rinse over the elderflowers to remove any dirt or little creatures. Pour the boiling water over the sugar in a very large mixing bowl. Stir well and leave to cool. Add the citric acid, the oranges and lemons sliced, and then the flowers. Leave in a cool place for 24 hours, stirring occasionally. Strain through muslin, pour into sterilised bottles.

Note: The citric acid is optional. If you use it, the cordial will keep for longer. The cordial can be frozen in ice-cube trays for future use. Diluted to taste, and processed in an ice-cream machine, it also makes a deliciously refreshing sorbet. Adventurous cooks might like to make elderflower fritters.

1 Tuesday

2 Wednesday   *Full Moon*

3 Thursday

4 Friday

5 Saturday

6 Sunday

Nuts in May

'…Nutkin was excessively impertinent in his manners.
He bobbed up and down like a little red cherry, singing
"Riddle me, riddle me, rot-tot-tote!
A little wee man in a red, red, coat!
A staff in his hand and a stone in his throat;
If you tell me this riddle, I'll give you a groat."
Beatrix Potter

7 Monday

Bank Holiday

8 Tuesday

9 Wednesday

10 Thursday

11 Friday

12 Saturday

13 Sunday

May was full of promises,
But she didn't keep them quick enough for some,
And a crowd of doubting Thomases
Was predicting that the summer'd never come.
But it's coming by gum, you can hear it come,
You can hear it in the trees, you can smell it on the breeze,
Look around, look around, look around!
Oscar Hammerstein Song from Carousel 1956

Painting by Lewis, 8

14 Monday

15 Tuesday

16 Wednesday   *New Moon*

17 Thursday

18 Friday

19 Saturday

20 Sunday

Queen Victoria

Victoria became Queen at the age of 18, and married Prince
Albert when she was 22. They had nine children and 41
grandchildren. Queen Victoria was 39 when her first grandchild
was born. When daughter Princess Victoria
(known in her family as Vicky) gave birth to a son, who
was to grow up to be Kaiser Wilhelm of Germany,
Queen Victoria wrote to her daughter:
*'[A] grandmother must ever be loved and venerated,
particularly one's mother's mother I always think.'*

Drawing by Chloe, 9

21 Monday

22 Tuesday   *22May-22 June* **Gemini**

23 Wednesday

24 Thursday   *1819 Queen Victoria's birthday*

25 Friday

26 Saturday

27 Sunday

Grannyblog

My Granny was a 'continental lady'. She moved to Britain,
to Worcestershire, from Vienna during the war, and totally
embraced her new life. She was a tiny, elegant figure, like a
little brown nut. My favourite thing with her was on
Sunday mornings when we used to have 'Tea in Bed'.
Granny would make a pot of tea and bring it up on a tray
with cups and saucers and milk and a tin of chocolate
marshmallow biscuits. When everything was ready, she
would call me and my sister in and we would get into
her big double bed where she would tell us stories
about our mum when she was little.

I really miss my mother, and in some ways I wish I had
made the effort to get her together with my children more
often. You only realise how much you miss them when
they are gone.

Grandchildren, are, I think, our reward for all that hard
work one put in bringing up our own children. They
make it all seem worth it.

I grew up without any grandparents, and always felt a
profound sense of lack as a result. My friends all seemed
to have wonderful, eccentric grandmothers who took
them to the theatre and sent them presents,
and I longed for one myself.

28 Monday *Bank Holiday*

29 Tuesday

30 Wednesday

31 Thursday *Full Moon*

June is busting out all over,
All over the meadows and the hills,
And the rams that chase the ewe sheep
Are predicting there'll be new sheep,
And the fish have got each other by the gills.
Because it's June, June, June, June, June.

June
2007

Coronation Day

This could be the cue to get out the dressing up box (all good grannies keep one!) for your grandchildren, and get them started playing Kings and Queens – there is a role for an archbishop too. If you haven't got old velvet curtains to use as cloaks, tablecloths will do. Help them make crowns and an orb and scepter with thin card, kitchen foil, a stapler, glue and glitter. If you go in for baubles, bangles and beads, get them out for the children to wear as a special treat.

Drawing by Sophie, 8

N.B. Be a good granny and take your grandchildren to see the Crown Jewels at the Tower of London. Grannies enjoy such trips, whereas parents often see them as a chore. A granny friend told me her best-ever outing with her grandson was to the Tower. Very energetic grannies could take in the London Eye and the Houses of Parliament on the same day as the Tower.

1 Friday

2 Saturday   *Queen Elizabeth II's Coronation Day 1953*

3 Sunday

Martha Washington

b 2 June 1731

When Martha Dandridge Custis met and married George
Washington, she was an attractive and wealthy widow of 28 with
two small children – her two older children having died. The
Washingtons brought up Jacky and Patsy Custis at their Mount
Vernon estate and never had children of their own. Although
Martha was pretty, lively and talkative, she never much enjoyed
the social responsibilities of her husband's political life, either
before or after he became President. She was happiest leading a
domestic life, writing to a friend that at home she was 'steady as a
clock, busy as a bee and cheerful as a cricket.' Illness and loss
clouded their happiness, Patsy dying of epilepsy when she was 17
and Jacky also dying young, having contracted a fever, probably
typhoid, at the Battle of Yorktown in 1781. When Jacky's widow
remarried, she took the two eldest of her four children with her
to her new home, but left the younger two, Nelly and Washy (also
known as Tub), with their grandparents, since Martha had been
heartbroken at the thought of losing all her grandchildren.
Martha loved having children in the house, and always made the
best of whatever life sent. She wrote, 'I am determined to be
cheerful and happy in whatever situation I may be. The greater
part of our happiness or misary [sic] depends on our dispositions
and not on our circumstances.' This was a remarkable philosophy
for a woman whose four children had died aged 3, 4, 17 and 27.
Her four grandchildren all grew to adulthood, three of them
reaching their seventies. All of them, and her seven great-grandchildren, were with Martha when she died at the age of 70.

4 Monday

5 Tuesday

6 Wednesday

7 Thursday

8 Friday

9 Saturday

10 Sunday

A Father's Day Cake

Make a plain or chocolate cake with your grandchildren.
Ice the cake and teach them how to decorate it, piping coloured
icing with a bag and nozzle to write a wobbly 'Dad'.

CLASSIC VICTORIA SPONGE

My grandmother and my mother made it, and I made it with
my children the hard way, using elbow grease to cream butter and
sugar and beat in the eggs. With my grandchildren we just whiz
all the ingredients in the food processor.

4 medium eggs
Weigh the eggs together and use the same weight of
Unsalted butter, softened
Caster Sugar
Self-raising flour
(for a chocolate cake, substitute 30g cocoa powder for 30g of the flour)
1 teaspoon vanilla extract
A little milk if needed.

Set the oven temp at 180°C/gas mark 4. Grease two 20cm
sandwich cake tins and line with baking parchment. Put all the
ingredients in the food processor and whiz until thoroughly
mixed. If the mixture seems too stiff, add milk a little at a time.
Divide between the two tins and bake in the preheated oven for
25 to 30 mins. After a few mins turn the cakes out on to a wire
rack. When cold, spread jam on one and, if you like, some
whipped cream Put the other cake on top and sprinkle caster
sugar or icing sugar over it. NB If you are making the chocolate
version, you can sandwich it with chocolate butter icing.

11 Monday

12 Tuesday

1819 Birthday of Charles Kingsley,
author of The Water Babies

13 Wednesday

14 Thursday

New Moon
Trooping the Colour (the Queen's official birthday)

15 Friday

1215 Magna Carta was signed by
King John at Runnymede

16 Saturday

17 Sunday

Father's Day

Picnic in the park

Now that it's summer, spend as much time as you can out of doors. Go to the park with your grandchildren, and take an old-fashioned teatime picnic: cucumber sandwiches, jam sandwiches, flapjacks and a punnet or two of strawberries, plus a flask of iced coffee or, if the children prefer it, chocolate milk. And stale bread for the ducks.

18 Monday

19 Tuesday

20 Wednesday

21 Thursday   *Summer Solstice, longest day*

22 Friday

23 Saturday   *23 June-23 July* **Cancer**

24 Sunday   *1650 Duke of Marlborough's birthday*

Henry VIII's Wives

He married them in this order:
Catherine of Aragon, Anne Boleyn, Jane Seymour,
Anne of Cleeves, Kathryn Howard, Katherine Parr.
Their fates were:
Divorced, Beheaded, Died; Divorced, Beheaded, Survived.

Drawing by Melissa, 9

25 Monday

26 Tuesday

27 Wednesday

28 Thursday   *1491 Henry VIII's birthday*

29 Friday

30 Saturday   *Full Moon*

July
2007

The Caucus-race
from Alice's Adventures in Wonderland
by Lewis Carroll

" ...They began running when they liked, and left
off when they liked, so that it was not easy to
know when the race was over. However, when they
had been running half an hour or so, and were quite
dry again, the Dodo suddenly called out 'The race
is over!' and they all crowded round it, panting,
and asking 'But who has won?'

This question the Dodo could not answer without
a great deal of thought... At last the Dodo said
'Everybody has won, and all must have prizes.'

Grannyblog

Grandmothers can be a vital source of support and confidence for their grandchildren. I remember when I was getting on very badly with my mum when I was a teenager, and it was my granny who seemed to understand. She never did my mum down, but just used to listen and offer the odd comment.

The person I remember almost more than my grandmother is 'Great Granny'. She lived in a very musty flat near the River Thames, and we used to go to tea often in the afternoon. There were always stale Rich Tea biscuits. And one day – I've never forgotten this – she said to me: 'It is not good to be vain, my girl. If you keep staring at yourself in that looking-glass, it will most definitely crack!'

Our Oma loved to moan about all our "beasts" when my brother and I came to stay. The "beasts" she was referring to were in fact our cuddly toys. I think she didn't really mind them too much – she always had a tear in her eye when it was time for all of us to leave.

1 Sunday

Independence Day

To celebrate independence from British rule, most towns in the USA have marching parades, with bands playing and baton-twirling drum majorettes prancing. It is a public holiday and a day for family get-togethers.
An evening fire-work display is part of the fun.

Yankee doodle came to town,
A-riding on a pony.
He stuck a feather in his cap
And called it Macaroni.

Painting by James, 9

2 Monday

3 Tuesday

4 Wednesday   *Independence Day USA*

5 Thursday

6 Friday

7 Saturday

8 Sunday

King Bruce and the Spider

King Bruce of Scotland flung himself down,
In a lowly mood to think;
'Tis true he was a monarch, and wore a crown,
But his heart was beginning to sink.

For he had been trying to do a great deed,
To make his people glad;
He had tried and tried, but could not succeed,
And so he became quite sad.

Now, just at that moment, the spider dropped
With its silken cobweb clew,
And the king, in the midst of his thinking stopped
To see what the spider would do.

It soon began to cling and crawl
Straight up with strong endeavour;
But down it came with a slipping sprawl,
As near to the ground as ever.

Again it fell, and swung below;
But up it quickly mounted,
Till up and down, now fast, now slow,
Nine brave attempts were counted.

Steadily, steadily, inch by inch,
Higher and higher he got,
And a bold little run, at the very last pinch,
Put him into the wished-for spot.

"Bravo, bravo!" the king cried out;
"All honour to those who try!
The spider up there defied despair;
he conquered, and why should not I."

July 2007

9 Monday

10 Tuesday

11 Wednesday

1271 King Robert I of Scotland's birthday (Robert the Bruce)

12 Thursday

13 Friday

14 Saturday

New Moon
Bastille Day

15 Sunday

St Swithin's Day

Going to the Pick-Your-Own

Strawberries, raspberries, red currants, blackcurrants: you can use
any or all of them in any proportion to make a traditional

SUMMER PUDDING
Serves 8
10oz/300g redcurrants
1lb/450g raspberries
4oz/170g caster sugar
1 tbsp water
a small piece of butter for greasing
5-6 slices stale white bread (with the crusts cut off)

Lightly butter a 1 pint pudding basin, and line it with the slices
of bread, cutting smaller slices to fill any gaps. The bread should
fit neatly and not overlap too much. Trim the bread so it is
flush with the top of the basin. Put $^1/_2$ of the fruit, with the
sugar and a little water, into a saucepan, and heat till the sugar
has dissolved and the juice begins to run. Add this to the rest
of the fruit. Pour the fruit mixture into the basin until it is
completely full but not overflowing. Cover with more slices
of bread, cut to fit, and place a plate on top of the
basin, with a weight on it to compress the pudding.
Leave for at least 5 hours, or overnight,
in the fridge. To serve the pudding,
remove the weight and plate, cover
the bowl with a serving plate and
invert to turn out the pudding. Serve
with thick cream or crème fraiche.

16 Monday

17 Tuesday

18 Wednesday

19 Thursday

20 Friday

21 Saturday

*Neil Armstrong was the first man
to walk on the moon 1969*

22 Sunday

How to Make a Sandboat

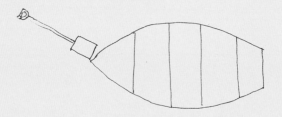

1. Draw the outline of the boat in the sand with the edge of a spade or with a stick.

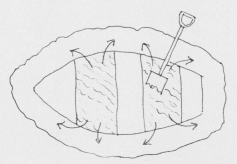

2. Dig out the sand between the seats and pile it up to make the sides. Pat them firm.

3. Get in the boat and wait for the tide to come in.

23 Monday

24 Tuesday

25 Wednesday

26 Thursday

27 Friday

28 Saturday   *1866 Beatrix Potter's birthday*

29 Sunday   *Full Moon*

Drawing by Sophie, 9

30 Monday

31 Tuesday

N.B. Check the local paper and parish notice boards for news about summer events. It's not all car boot sales and beer festivals: in many parts of the country you can still find traditional fêtes where you can bowl for a pig, guess the weight of the cake, shy a ball at a coconut, and buy bath salts past their sell-by date on a White Elephant stall. There might even be a Fancy Dress contest for the children to enter. Who better than granny to get creative with their costumes?

August
2007

I do like to be beside the seaside!
Oh, I do like to be beside the sea!
I do like to stroll along the prom, prom, prom,
While the brass band plays tiddleyompompom!

Oh, just let me be beside the seaside!
I'll be beside myself with glee.
There are lots of girls besides,
That I'd like to be beside,
Beside the seaside, beside the sea.

Queen Elizabeth the Queen Mother

b 4 August 1900

For many years of her long life (she died aged 101) the Queen Mum was Britain's favourite granny. Here is the tribute of Prince Charles, the oldest of her six grandchildren, and, by all accounts, the closest:

'I know what my darling grandmother meant to so many other people. She was the original life enhancer, whether publicly or privately, whoever she was with. And, in many ways, she had become an institution in her own right, a presence in the nation and in other realms and territories beyond these shores. At once indomitable, somehow timeless, able to span the generations; wise, loving, and an utterly irresistible mischievousness of spirit; an immensely strong character, combined with a unique natural grace, and an infectious optimism about life itself. Above all, she understood the British character and her heart belonged to this ancient land and its equally indomitable and humorous inhabitants, whom she served with panache, style and unswerving dignity for very nearly 80 years. For me, she meant everything and I had dreaded, dreaded this moment along with, I know, countless others. She seemed gloriously unstoppable and, since I was a child, I adored her. She was quite simply the most magical grandmother you could possibly have. Her departure has left an irreplaceable chasm in countless lives but, thank God, we are all the richer for the sheer joy of her presence and everything she stood for.'

N.B. For summer treats make healthy ice lollies with fruit juice. Just pour the juice into plastic lolly moulds, put a stick in each one, and freeze. Try making striped lollies, frozen yoghurt or ice cream lollies. The children can help (or hinder).

1 Wednesday

2 Thursday

3 Friday

4 Saturday

5 Sunday

Beach-Combing

Seaweed, shells, pebbles, cuttlefish, empty crab legs, tide-smoothed glass, driftwood 'dragons'… all sorts of treasures can be collected along the tide line. On a rainy day, glue sand, shells and seaweed onto stiff card to make a collage picture of the sea shore. When the tide is out, plump mussels can be picked off the rocks and cooked for a few moments with wine, garlic and parsley to make moules marinière.

6 Monday

7 Tuesday

8 Wednesday

9 Thursday

10 Friday

11 Saturday

12 Sunday   *New Moon*

A Day At The Seaside.

One day while we were in Wales staying in a caravan, we got invited by our friends to go in their motor boat to a very small beach which you could not reach by car as it was surrounded by cliffs on 2 sides and the other sides were open to the sea.

When we got to the me beach, my friend and I made a boat out of sand and several barriers against the sea, to protect it. Then we blew up their rubber dinghy and let the waves lift in it up. Then we saw that the sea was almost upon our sand boat so we all sat in it auntil it had collapsed. Then we had our lunch which was sardine sandwiches and ribena to drink.

After luch our Mothers thought it was time to go back so we dried ourselves and put our clothes on.

by Philippa, 9

13 Monday

14 Tuesday

15 Wednesday

16 Thursday

17 Friday

18 Saturday

19 Sunday

Water Play

If you have small children to entertain on a warm summer's day, and you have a garden, fill the largest plastic bowl you can find with warm water and put it outside, somewhere you can keep an eye on them. Provide the children with plastic cups, spoons, and sieves and they will play happily while you get on with your chores. A word of caution: this works best on paving – on grass you risk turning your lawn into a mud-bath.

20 Monday

21 Tuesday

22 Wednesday

23 Thursday

24 Friday   *24 August-23 September Virgo*

25 Saturday

26 Sunday

Cut-Away Dancers

1. Fold a strip of paper like a concertina

2. Draw half a dancer, making sure the arms
reach to the edge of the papers

3. Cut away surplus paper

4. Unfold and decorate as you wish

27 Monday *Bank Holiday*

___

28 Tuesday *Full Moon*

___

29 Wednesday

___

30 Thursday

___

31 Friday

___

N.B. If you have a grandchild starting school next term and he or she is a little apprehensive, now is the time to give Lauren Child's funny and reassuring book *I am too absolutely small for school.*

September 2007

Back to School – Things to do:
Sew on name tapes ✓
Buy football boots for M. ✓
Find G's lunch box ✓
Wash PE kit ✓
Mend pencil case ✓
Buy geometry set ✓
Get hair cut ✓

The Fire of London

The fire started in Pudding Lane and lasted 5 days,
destroying most of the city.

The diarist Samuel Pepys watched from a boat on the Thames:
'The streets full of nothing but people and horses and carts
laden with goods, ready to run over one another. In the evening,
when we could endure no more upon the water, we landed at
Bankside, Southwark, at a small public house, and there stood
and saw the fire grown, and as it grew darker appeared more and
more, and in corners and upon steeples, and between churches
and houses, as far as we could see up the City, in a most horrid
bloody malicious flame, not like the flame of an ordinary fire.'

Another eye witness was John Evelyn:
'God grant mine eyes may never behold the like, who now saw
above 10,000 houses all in one flame; the noise and cracking
and thunder of the impetuous flames, the shrieking of women
and children, the hurry of people, the fall of tower, horses and
churches, was like an hideous storm.'

It seems miraculous that only 9 people died.

The Great Fire is commemorated by a small statue of a boy in
Cock Lane near Pie Corner where the fire is said to have ended.
Sir Christopher Wren's landmark Monument is 200 feet from
the site of the hose in Pudding Lane where it started.

N.B. Sir Christopher Wren said
"I'm going to dine with some men.
If anyone calls,
Tell them I'm designing St Paul's."
Edward Clerihew Bentley.

If it wasn't for the Fire of London we wouldn't have St Paul's Cathedral. A visit to St Paul's followed by a walk across 'the wobbly bridge' to Tate Modern, then a river boat trip (a rest for granny), makes a great day out in the capital for older children.

1 Saturday

2 Sunday   *1666 The Great Fire of London*

Grandma Moses
b. 7 September 1860

An inspiration to all grandmothers, Grandma Moses, born
Anna Mary Robertson in New York State, USA, became, in her
eighties, a famous painter in the naïve style. She was one of ten
children in a Scottish-Irish farming family, and learned as a girl
to cook, clean, sew and make soap and candles. At 27 she
married Thomas Salmon Moses and the couple went to farm
in the Shenandoah valley and later, back in New York State.
Their life was hard working but satisfying, and Grandma
Moses only started painting after her husband died, when she
was already in her late seventies. She painted what she called
'Old timey things', happy scenes of farming and family life from
her childhood. She was amazed by her own commercial success.
'Anybody can paint,' she said, and 'If I didn't start painting I
would have raised chickens. I'm not one to sit back in a rocking
chair, waiting for someone to help.'
Whatever the secret of longevity is (a healthy outdoor life,
perhaps, or a happy disposition), Grandma Moses had it. She
lived to 101, and had 11 grandchildren and 10 great-
grandchildren. The great-grandchildren, she said, were
even more fun than the grandchildren had been.

3 Monday

4 Tuesday

5 Wednesday

6 Thursday

1620 The Mayflower sailed from Plymouth taking the Pilgrim Fathers to America

7 Friday

1533 Queen Elizabeth I was born

8 Saturday

9 Sunday

Blackberrying

'Flopsy, Mopsy and Cottontail,
who were good little bunnies,
went down the lane to gather blackberries.'
The Tale of Peter Rabbit, by Beatrix Potter.

Get your blackberry picking done in September;
after this month they are supposed to taste bad
because the devil has pissed on them.
As a change from Blackberry and Apple
Pie, and Bramble Jelly, try sieving out the
pips and making a delicately flavoured
mousse, ice cream or sorbet.

10 Monday

11 Tuesday   *New Moon*

12 Wednesday

13 Thursday   *1916 Roald Dahl's birthday*

14 Friday

15 Saturday

16 Sunday   *1387 Henry V's birthday*

The Game of Conkers

The best conkers to play with are uncracked, firm and symmetrical. Make a hole through the middle of your chosen conker. Thread a strong piece of string, about 25cm long, through the hole and tie a knot at one end, so that it doesn't pull through. Each player has a conker hanging on its string. Players take turns at hitting their opponent's conker. If a player misses, he is allowed up to two further goes. If the strings tangle, the first player to call 'strings' gets an extra shot. If a player drops his conker, or it is knocked out of his hand, the other player can shout 'stamps' and jump on it; but, should its owner first cry 'no stamps', then the conker, hopefully, remains intact. The game goes on in turns until one or other of the two conkers is completely destroyed.

17 Monday

---

18 Tuesday

---

19 Wednesday

---

20 Thursday

---

21 Friday

---

22 Saturday

---

23 Sunday

HMS Victory

Nelson's (nearly) last words, 'Kiss me, Hardy,' spoken as he lay dying, on his flagship *HMS Victory*, are among the most famous ever. A moment before, he had said, 'Take care of my dear Lady Hamilton, Hardy, take care of poor Lady Hamilton.' After Hardy kissed him on the cheek, Nelson said, 'Now I am satisfied. Thank God I have done my duty.' Those really were his last words, and Hardy then knelt and kissed the Admiral again, on the forehead. Today you can visit *HMS Victory* in Portsmouth Docks. For opening times, go to www.HMS-Victory.com.

Drawing by William, 7

September 2007

24 Monday

25 Tuesday

26 Wednesday

Full Moon

27 Thursday

28 Friday

29 Saturday

1738 Horatio Nelson was born

30 Sunday

*1788 Lord Raglan's Birthday. He was responsible
for The Charge of the Light Brigade*

October 2007

O wild West Wind, thou breath of Autumn's being
Thou from whose unseen presence the leaves dead
Are driven like ghosts from an enchanter fleeing,

Yellow, and black, and pale, and hectic red,
Pestilence-stricken multitudes! O thou
Who chariotest to their dark wintry bed
The winged seeds, where they lie cold and low,
Each like a corpse within its grave, until
Thine azure sister of the Spring shall blow

Her clarion o'er the dreaming earth, and fill
(Driving sweet buds like flocks to feed in air)
With living hues and odours plain and hill;

Wild spirit, which art moving everywhere;
Destroyer and preserver: hear, O hear!

Ode to the West Wind, verse I, by Percy Bysshe Shelley

Autumn Leaves

The leaves are beginning to colour and fall. Small children like to collect as many different kinds and colours as they can find. Over-sixes can take leaf 'rubbings'. Choose leaves with a strong pattern of raised veins and place each one, veins uppermost, on a sheet of paper. Cover it with another, thin sheet, and rub evenly with a soft pencil or crayon. Leaves can be pressed, like flowers, between two sheets of blotting paper, under a pile of heavy books.

October 2007

1 Monday

2 Tuesday

3 Wednesday

4 Thursday

5 Friday

6 Saturday

7 Sunday

The Bayeux Tapestry

King Harold II was killed at the Battle of Hastings, probably by an arrow in his eye as shown on the Bayeux tapestry. A trip to Normandy to see the tapestry would make a fantastic treat for grandchildren of, say, 10 and over. Next best: an outing to see the replica at Reading Museum, Berkshire.
(www.bayeuxtapestry.org.uk)

8 Monday

9 Tuesday

10 Wednesday   *New Moon*

11 Thursday

12 Friday

13 Saturday

14 Sunday   *1066 Death of Harold II at*
                               the Battle of Hastings

Elinor Glyn's grandmother

(Elinor Glyn b 17 Oct 1864)

Elinor Glyn, a beautiful red-head, became famous as the
writer of steamy, romantic novels in the early years of the
20th century. She invented 'It' as a code-word for Sex
Appeal. She was born Elinor Sutherland in Jersey, but
was partly brought up in Canada and England by her
French grandmother. The description in her book
Reflections of Ambrosine (1903) was probably
based on her own grandmother:

'Grandmamma was eighty-eight last July! No one would think
it to look at her; She is not deaf or blind or any of
those annoying things, and she sits bolt-upright in her chair, and
her face is not very wrinkled – more like fine, old, white kid.
Her hair is arranged with such a chic; it is white…
her eyes are the eyes of a hawk, the proudest eyes I have
ever seen. Her third and little fingers are bent with rheumatism,
but she still polishes her nails and covers the
rest of her hands with mittens. You can't exactly love
grandmamma, but you feel you respect her dreadfully,
and it is a great honour when she is pleased…
Grandmamma has given me most of my education herself
since we came to England, and she has been especially particular
about deportment. I have never been allowed to lean back in my
chair or loll on a sofa and she has taught me how to go in and
out of a room and how to enter a carriage…
There are three things, she says, a woman ought to look –
straight as a dart, supple as a snake, and proud as a tiger-lily.

15 Monday

16 Tuesday

17 Wednesday

18 Thursday

19 Friday

20 Saturday   *1632 Sir Christopher Wren born*

21 Sunday   *1805 Battle of Trafalgar*
                                   and the death of Nelson

Winter Draws In

Putting the clocks back means long, cosy evenings snuggled
up on the sofa with a book, or watching a video or DVD.
Take the opportunity to introduce your grandchildren
to some of your own favourites, or let them make
their own choice at the library.

22 Monday

23 Tuesday

24 Wednesday

24 October-22 November Scorpio

25 Thursday

Full Moon

26 Friday

27 Saturday

28 Sunday

British summer time ends. Clocks back, extra hour in bed.

Making a Pumpkin Lantern

1. Cut a circular hole around the stalk of the pumpkin. Tilt the point of the knife into the centre of the pumpkin. This will stop the lid from falling in.

2. Scoop out the seeds and any loose flesh using a dessertspoon and a knife.

3. Sketch the face onto your pumpkin. Use a biro so any mistakes can be scrubbed off with a scouring pad or fingernail.

4. Carefully cut out the features. Take small cuts and use a puncturing motion rather than a slicing one. Gently scrape away the flesh on the inside of the face until it is only 1 cm thick.

5. Using the knife, mark a circle the size of your candle or tea-light in the centre of the base. Carefully hollow out the marked area with the teaspoon and place your candle in the hollow; light it, and replace the lantern lid.

October 2007

29 Monday

30 Tuesday

*1925 John Logie Baird made the first
TV transmission of a moving image*

31 Wednesday

Halloween

November

2007

Remember, remember, the fifth of November,
Gunpowder treason and plot.
I see no reason why gunpowder treason
Should ever be forgot.

Granny Smith
exact d.o.b. not known

The only Granny to
have an apple named after her! Mary Ann
Sherwood was born at Peasmarsh, Sussex, in 1799
and married Thomas Smith when she was 19.
In 1838 they and their five surviving children
emigrated to New South Wales in Australia.
After a spell working on an estate at Ryde, the Smiths
bought 24 acres of their own land and started an orchard.
The famous brilliant green, crisp, juicy apple appeared
among some French crab apples growing beside a creek on
the farm. Sadly neither Mary Ann nor Thomas lived to
see their apple's commercial success (she died in 1870).
'Granny Smith's seedlings' won the prize for cooking
apples at Castle Hill Agricultural and Horticultural
Show in 1891, and several growers began
cultivating the Granny Smith
apple and, in due course,
exporting it.

by Thomas, 8

November 2007

Apple bobbing is a traditional party game. Float apples in
a bucket or washing-up bowl of cold water. Each player has
to get an apple out of the water, with hands clasped behind
his back, using only his teeth. Small apples are easier than
big ones. Put a towel on the floor, have another towel handy
to mop each child and, if possible, a set of dry clothes each.

1 Thursday

2 Friday

3 Saturday

4 Sunday

BONFIRE NIGHT

In 1605 thirteen conspirators, led by Robert Catesby, plotted to blow up King James I and the Houses of Parliament. One of the conspirators wrote to a friend , warning him to stay away from Parliament. His letter reached the king and, on 5 November, a search was made and Guy Fawkes was found in a cellar beneath the House of Lords, with 36 barrels of gunpowder. The arrest of Guy Fawkes and the prevention of the plot are commemorated every year with fireworks and bonfires on which his effigy is burned.

LESTER PIGGOTT

One of the most famous English jockeys ever. Lester rode his first winner aged 12 in 1948, was champion jockey 11 times and won the Derby 9 times.

'DR LIVINGSTONE, I PRESUME'

The American journalist Henry Morton Stanley is said to have greeted the Scottish missionary and explorer Dr David Livingstone with these words, when they met on the shores of Lake Tanganyika.

November 2007

5 Monday

1605 The gunpowder Plot
1935 Lester Piggott's birthday

---

6 Tuesday

---

7 Wednesday

---

8 Thursday

---

9 Friday

New Moon

---

10 Saturday

1871 Henry Morton Stanley met
David Livingstone

---

11 Sunday

Remembrance Day (Poppy Day)

Lady Russell

b 15 Nov 1814

Frances Anna Maria Elliot became the second wife of Lord John Russell who was to serve twice as Prime Minister. She was brought up as a Scottish Presbyterian, later became a Unitarian and remained rather austerely religious all her life. Her husband's parliamentary colleagues referred to her as 'Deadly Nightshade' but her grandson Bertrand Russell wrote that, 'She never lost a certain kind of gaiety.' Bertrand Russell, who became a great philosopher and mathematician was brought up by this remarkable grandmother from the age of two and educated by her, after the deaths of his father, mother and sister. She could speak French, German and Italian faultlessly, was familiar with the classical literature in those languages, and knew Shakespeare, Milton and the 18th-century poets intimately. Nevertheless Bertrand Russell wrote, 'After I reached the age of fourteen my grandmother's intellectual limitations became trying to me, and her Puritan morality began to seem to me to be excessive; but while I was a child her great affection for me, and her intense care for my welfare, made me love her and gave me that feeling of safety that children need. As I have grown older, I have realized more and more the importance she had in moulding my outlook on life. Her fearlessness, her public spirit, her contempt for convention have always seemed good to me.'

November 2007

12 Monday

1035 *Death of King Canute*

13 Tuesday

14 Wednesday

15 Thursday

16 Friday

17 Saturday

18 Sunday

Pumpkin Pie

When Americans gather anywhere in the world for Thanksgiving,
the traditional feast includes roast turkey with cranberry sauce,
followed by Pumpkin Pie (which is actually more of a tart).

1 medium sugar pumpkin
1 tbs vegetable oil
1 nine-inch frozen pastry case for single crust pie
$^1/_2$ tsp ground ginger
$^1/_2$ tsp ground cinnamon
1 tbs dark rum
1 tsp salt
4 eggs, lightly beaten
1 cup honey, warmed slightly
$^1/_2$ cup milk
$^1/_2$ cup heavy whipping cream
$^1/_2$ cup chopped pecans

Cut pumpkin in half, and remove seeds. Lightly oil the cut
surface. Place cut side down on a jelly roll pan lined with foil
and lightly oiled. Bake at 325 °F. until the flesh is tender. Cool
until just warm. Scrape the pumpkin flesh from the peel. Either
mash, or puree, in small batches in a blender. In a large bowl,
mix together 2 cups pumpkin puree, the spices and salt. Beat in
eggs, rum, honey, milk and cream. Pour filling into pie shell.
Bake at 400 °F for 50 to 55 minutes, or until a knife inserted
1 inch from the edge of the pie comes out clean. Cool on a wire
rack and store in refrigerator until ready to serve – with
whipped cream and a light dusting of cinnamon.

19 Monday

20 Tuesday

21 Wednesday

22 Thursday   *Thanksgiving Day USA*

23 Friday   *23 November-22 December* **Sagittarius**

24 Saturday   *Full Moon*

25 Sunday

The Tiger

by William Blake

Tiger, tiger, burning bright
In the forests of the night,
What immortal hand or eye
Could frame thy fearful symmetry?

In what distant deeps or skies
Burnt the fire of thine eyes?
On what wings dare he aspire?
What the hand dare seize the fire?

And what shoulder and what art
Could twist the sinews of thy heart?
And when thy heart began to beat,
What dread hand and what dread feet?

What the hammer? What the chain?
In what furnace was thy brain?
What the anvil? What dread grasp
Dare its deadly terrors clasp?

When the stars threw down their spears,
And water'd heaven with their tears,
Did He smile His work to see?
Did He who made the lamb make thee?

Tiger, tiger, burning bright
In the forests of the night,
What immortal hand or eye
Dare frame thy fearful symmetry?

November 2007

26 Monday

*1922 In Egypt Howard Carter and Lord
Caernarvon got their first glimpse into
Tutankhamen's tomb.*

---

27 Tuesday

---

28 Wednesday

1757 William Blake's birthday

---

29 Thursday

---

30 Friday

St Andrew's Day

N.B. If you are planning to take grandchildren to a pantomime, play or circus, book early to avoid disappointment. The show put on by locals in the Parish Hall can often be just as much fun as an extravagant theatre production starring TV soap stars.

December 2007

Christmas is coming and the geese are getting fat.
Please put a penny in the old man's hat.
If you haven't got a penny, a halfpenny will do,
If you haven't got a halfpenny, God bless you.

Card by Lucy, 9

Get out the glue and glitter and help your
grandchildren make d-i-y Christmas cards
and calendars. The weekend colour supplements in
the run-up to Christmas are full of festive imagery,
beautifully wrapped presents and snowy scenes, ideal
for cutting and sticking. Buy envelopes of a good size
and cut the cards to fit them. And perhaps even check
out the Royal Mail's special Christmas stamps.

For other ways to get in the mood, visit Santa's grotto
(take the grandchildren, too, of course!) – Kew Gardens
have one of the best (1 Dec-2 Jan).
Alternatively, watch *The Polar Express* on DVD.

---

1 Saturday

---

2 Sunday *First Sunday in Advent*

Father Christmas

Help your grandchildren write their letters to Father Christmas telling him how good they've been all year and what presents they would like. Traditionally the letters were sent up the chimney, but you can always walk to the letterbox with an envelope addressed to *The North Pole*. (Make sure you remember the contents of the letter!)

Dear father christmas,
i want to have some
speshil pens and some
slipers and a piggy
Bank and please can
i have the last thing
as a suprise,
thankyou.

from Esther

3 Monday

4 Tuesday

5 Wednesday

6 Thursday

7 Friday

*1783 William Pitt the Younger became the youngest
ever Prime Minister aged 24.
1761 Madame Tussaud's birthday.*

8 Saturday

9 Sunday

New Moon

The Nativity Play

Jack had a crush on the little girl playing Mary, and wanted to play Joseph, but he was given the part of the Innkeeper. When Mary and Joseph arrived at the Inn, and asked if there was any room, he replied, 'Mary can come in, but Joseph needs to find somewhere else.'

If you get a chance to watch a grandchild perform, stock up on tissues. The chances are it will bring a tear to your eye to see your darling on stage as a shepherd, an angel, or a snowflake. Most schools have to restrict the audience numbers per family, so don't be too disappointed if this year it's the other granny's turn.

December 2007

10 Monday

11 Tuesday

12 Wednesday

13 Thursday

14 Friday

15 Saturday

16 Sunday

1773 The Boston Tea Party

A White Christmas?

I'm dreaming of a white Christmas
Just like the ones I used to know
Where the tree tops glisten
And children listen
To hear the sleigh bells in the snow

I'm dreaming of a white Christmas
With every Christmas card I write
May your days be merry and bright
And may all your Christmases be white

December 2007

17 Monday

18 Tuesday

19 Wednesday

20 Thursday

21 Friday

22 Saturday

Winter solstice – Shortest Day

23 Sunday

*23 December-19 January **Capricorn***
New Moon

On Christmas Eve...

Children hang up stockings.
Don't forget a drink and mince pie for Father Christmas
and something for his reindeer.

...On Boxing Day, good grannies keep the children
occupied while the parents nurse their hangovers. Lay in
a stock of batteries for the new toys and gadgets, and try
and get them outdoors for fresh air and exercise.

December 2007

24 Monday   *Christmas Eve*

25 Tuesday   *Christmas Day*

26 Wednesday   *Boxing Day / St Stephen's Day*

27 Thursday

28 Friday

29 Saturday

30 Sunday   *1865 Rudyard Kipling's birthday*

Dear Granny and grandpa.
Thank you for the music
stand and the spirograph
I am velly engoeing it so
much.

Love from Max.

December 2007

New Year's Eve, Hogmanay
You have seen in enough new years not to
mind staying home baby-sitting just this once!

Parents who have difficulty persuading their children to sit down and write their thank-you letters should send for Super-gran. She will make the chore seem like fun, sitting down with them and chatting about who gave them what, and what they would like to say in their letters. If they find writing very difficult, she will encourage them to draw a picture to show their thanks, and guide their pen round the letters of HAPPY NEW YEAR.

Clearing Up

After the festivities are over, don't be too quick to throw
all the wrapping away – often children prefer the boxes to
the expensive gifts that they contained.

1 Tuesday *New Years Day*

2 Wednesday

3 Thursday

4 Friday

5 Saturday

6 Sunday

Good Granny Gallery

I Love my granma Because
She Lives in The
contryside and
has two dogs.
my grandad
teches me gaimg
She cooks delisoos
meals. we go
Oh very Long
Walks.

by Eliza, 5

My Nonna

My name is Elena. My Nonna comes from Italy and cooks delicious food. Her real name is Annina but everyone calls her Anna. Every year we visit her in Italy. She gives us lots of presents even when it is not our birthday. She is very cuddly and takes us out for dinner. Her birthday is on the 5th November and makes us lots of clothes. In Italy she sometimes speaks in Italian so we don't know what she is saying. My Nonna is the best Nonna in the world and no-one could replace her.

My Nonna

by Elena

Grandpa by Guy, 4

My granny never wastes food even when its way past its sell-by-date. She also runs my bath with exactly 2 inches of water. She is really nice and always buying me sweats.

by Adam, 10

My Granny

My name is Layla. I love my Granny because she does everything for me. If my mum says, "No, you can't," my Granny says, "Yes you can." When Granny visits she takes me to lots of fun places like Theme Parks, the cinema e.t.c. She has a very nice smile and laugh which makes me think of nice things. When I'm bored she asks me if I want to play a game or go to the park for a picnic. When my sister and I fight she doesn't shout, she just calms us down nicely. She buys me lots of presents and teaches me lots of things.

by Layla

MAX

Grandpa

Granny

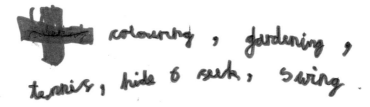

I do at Granny & Grandpas house ....

colouring , gardening ,
tennis, hide & seek, swing .

Good Granny Gallery

My granny

Hi my name is Sophie and my granny is the best in the world. Her name is Julia but I call her nanny. She comes round to my house every two months, and likes to give me and my sister sweets and chocolates. She cooks delicious food and I love her. I am named after my nanny Julia because my mum and dad like her name so much. She is 66 and her birthday is on the 1st of June. I love my nanny because she is kind to me. I also love her because she takes me places, often when we are not expecting it. She is my dad's mum and she loves me like she loves my dad. I love her because she loves me more than anything in the world.

By Sophie. Cassar

My Granny

My Granny's name is Nelanie. She is 72 years old. She likes shopping. She used to like sports. She was a Netball Captain. She is the oldest in our family and I'm the youngest.

I love my granny because she teaches me Netball when I go and visit her in Sri-lanka. I sometimes miss her because she is right the way in Sri-lanka. She is very funny and, even though she sometimes gets annoyed with me, I still love her.

By Nawani wickramaratne
age : 9

G rannies are good things to have.
R iots are ofter started by grannies.
A nd occasionly riots are not.
N othing replaces a granny.
N o granny is the same
I t's always important to have a granny on your side.
E nding grannies would be like ending the world.
S mall, they are, timid, they're not.

by Reddy, 12

My Grandma is the most kind and special grandma in the whole wide world. She takes me to the park, helps me in the garden and buys me presents.
I love my grandma.

Hanna Ellisson age 6

Good Granny Gallery

★★★ My grandma ★ ★ ★ ★ ★ ★

My Grandma is called Mary and I like her because she's:-

Fun.

good at telling jokes

Kind

has a good sense of humour

Smiley

always got time for me

She makes me smile

She's good at chatting.

I love my Grandma, She's great!

My Grandma is on my Dads' side, and comes from Middlesborough. My Grandma doesn't like middlesborough football matches as much as my Dad does though!

by Hannah

Good Granny Gallery

Good Granny Gallery

my granny has eyes. She Likes making pies and
she Lies in bed at night. my granny wears glasses
and she Likes to play pusses and her glasses are circles. my granny
Likes to take part in Art and she makes jolly good art as
vell

by Stella, 7

Good Granny Gallery

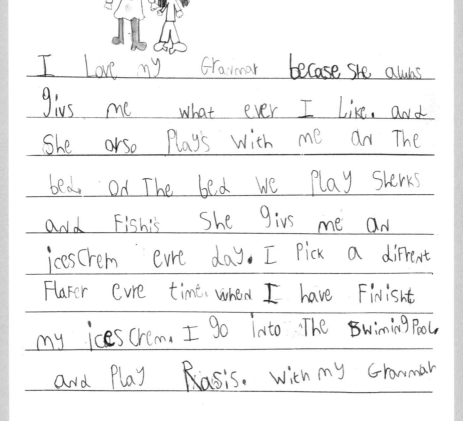

I Love my Granmar becase she alwas givs me what ever I Like, and she arso Plays with me an the bed. On the bed we Play sherks and Fishis She givs me an icescrem evre Day. I Pick a diffrent Flaver evre time. when I have Finisht my icescrem. I go into the Bwiming Pool and Play Rasis. with my Granmah

by Joely, 6

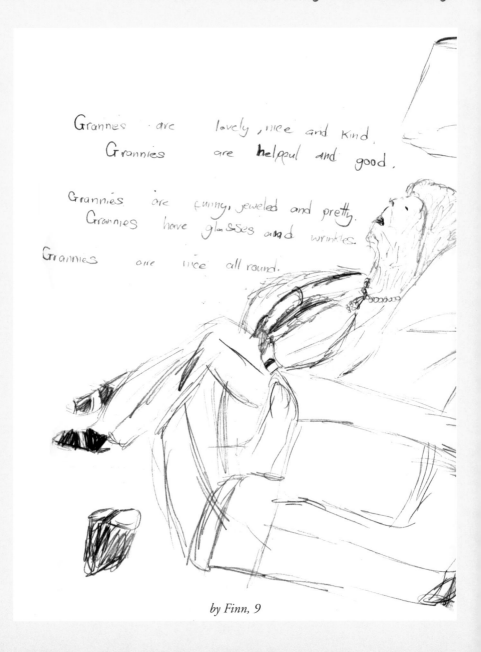

Grannies are lovely, nice and kind.
Grannies are helpful and good.

Grannies are funny, jeweled and pretty.
Grannies have glasses and wrinkles.
Grannies are nice all round.

by Finn, 9

My Grandma

My name is Ziana
I love my Grandma because she is sweet, friendly,
likes playing random games and slapping hand games.

My Grandma is chubby, not skinny like my Grandfather,
I like hugging my Grandma a lot. She has a big wide
face with a huge smile, kind eyes. She smiles nearly
all the time. Her shiny black long hair is nearly up to
knees. My Grandma is the best especially when
we play games.

by Ziana

My Grandma

My grandma was 81 when she died. She lived in Australia so I only saw her every two years. What I liked about her was that whenever I was with my other brother and sister she would call be curly because I had curly hair.

She was the best grandma in the world and I will never forget her.

By Lara

Good Granny Gallery

I Love my granny
because she taks me
enywer I want. but
my granndad dide so
I can't see him
eny day or eny
weekend. and I
went to a phyonrou
and we sendid sum
blons of to him.
but I cride a bit.

by Poppy

Good Granny Gallery

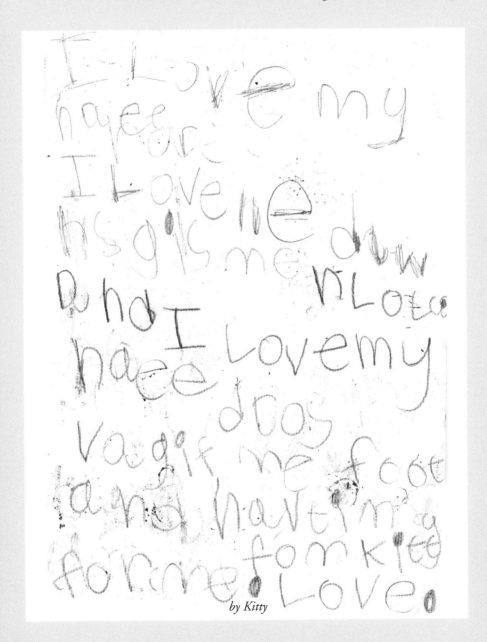

I Love my
nagee ...
I Love ne
his gis me draw
and I ... nLota
nagee I Love my
d dog
va gif me foot
and have my
for me fom kie
Love

by Kitty

Good Granny Gallery

I I like my grandmar because she reeds to me. She Even sym tims tacks me to the park. Its very nise for me to get abit of fresh ere But soon she is gowing to Diey But I still have got my mumy

by Loura

My Granny

I love my granny because she's funny and has got a very cute dog called Rosie, who scares my sister when she barks. Sometimes she invites me on my own, which is fun because she lets me go to the park for an hour, which mummy doesn't let me do! I also love my granny because she cooks me really nice meals.

By Charlotte Inskip

age: 9½

Granny

Rosie →

me

My Grandma

My Grandma is called Kerry,
I love her very, very, very much.
One of the reasons why I love
my Grandma is she gives all the
things I like, like chocolate
and sweets.

by Katrina
Messina

I like my
granny because
she hids choclet
evree time I
cum to her hous.

by Lily

Granny Jane and Grandpa I love you so much

Love from Max and Guy

Jane Fearnley-Whittingstall, author of the bestselling *Good Granny Guide*, has written many other books on plants and gardening, including *Gardening Made Easy* and Peonies – *The Imperial Flower*. A grandmother of five, and the mother of TV chef Hugh, she lives with her husband in Gloucestershire.

In case of difficulty in purchasing any
Short Books title through normal channels,
please contact BOOKPOST
Tel: 01624 836000
Fax: 01624 837033
Email: bookshop@enterprise.net
www.bookpost.co.uk
Please quote ref. 'Short Books'